MONSTER MATH
Puzzles and Games
WORKBOOK, BOOK TWO

Ages 6 to 8

By Oksana Hlodan
Illustrated by Yvonne Cherbak

LOWELL HOUSE JUVENILE

LOS ANGELES

NTC/Contemporary Publishing Group

For Kinga Wiater, who loves to learn and solve problems.
—O.H.

Reviewed and endorsed by Ronn Yablun, author of
Mathamazement and **How to Develop Your Child's
Gifts and Talents in Math**

Published by Lowell House
A division of NTC/Contemporary Publishing Group, Inc.
4255 West Touhy Avenue, Lincolnwood (Chicago), Illinois 60646-1975 U.S.A.

Managing Director and Publisher: Jack Artenstein
Director of Publishing Services: Rena Copperman
Editorial Director: Brenda Pope-Ostrow
Director of Art Production: Bret Perry
Editor: Linda Gorman

Lowell House books can be purchased at special discounts when
ordered in bulk for premiums and special sales.
Please contact Customer Service at:
NTC/Contemporary Publishing Group
4255 W. Touhy Avenue
Lincolnwood, IL 60646-1975
1-800-323-4900

Printed and bound in the United States of America

ISBN: 0-7373-0147-3

10 9 8 7 6 5 4 3 2

Note to Parents

Monster Math is a wonderful learning tool that will introduce your child to math. A community of lovable monsters teach and present the activities in this workbook, helping your child acquire a solid foundation in cognitive and deductive reasoning, problem solving, and analytical thinking. What a great way to build skills and instill a love of learning!

The activities in this workbook contain a range of difficulty levels, from basic addition and subtraction to beginning multiplication, division, and fractions. It is important that your child complete the activities in order, since the workbook progresses from simple visual discrimination to more advanced problem solving. Skipping activities that appear early in the workbook may cause frustration with later ones.

Let your child work at his or her own pace—four to five pages at a time may be enough for one sitting. After each activity is completed, have your child turn to the back of the workbook to check the answers. If an answer is incorrect, review the problem together. When discussing an incorrect answer, be positive and supportive. Talk about how your child arrived at the incorrect answer. Perhaps he or she simply did not understand what was expected. Make sure your child understands the problem completely before moving on to the next activity.

Written by an educator and endorsed by a teacher of mathematics, **Monster Math** will benefit any child who has a desire to learn. Once your child has completed the book, try creating new monster story problems for him or her to solve. You may discover that your child loves learning math—and has the skills to prove it!

A MONSTER WELCOME

Rodney, on the left, and Ursula, on the right, have a message for you. Find the message by coloring in:

- All of the boxes in Rodney's last column.
- The top box in Rodney's first column.
- The middle box in Ursula's bottom row.
- The second and third boxes in Rodney's middle row.
- The top three boxes in Ursula's middle column.
- The rest of the boxes in Rodney's first column.

Hint: Columns go up and down. **Rows** go across.

HUNGRY MONSTERS

The monsters are checking the refrigerator for snacks. Fill in the chart below to show how much food they find. Use a crayon to color one square for each item of food.

	1	2	3	4	5	6	7	8	9	10
bananas										
pineapples										
juice boxes										
apples										

JAG'S PATTERN BLOCKS

Jag is making **patterns** with his building blocks. A pattern is a design that is repeated over and over. Continue each pattern by drawing more blocks. Make sure the shapes you draw follow Jag's pattern. The first one is done for you.

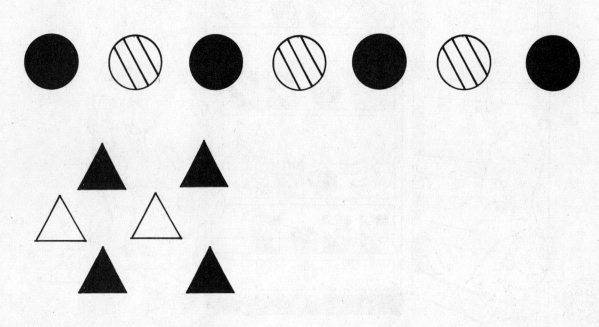

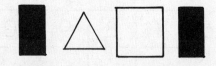

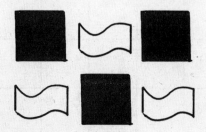

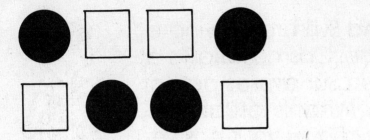

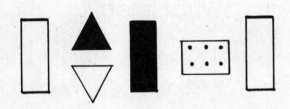

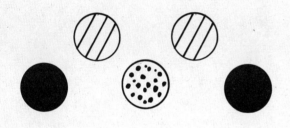

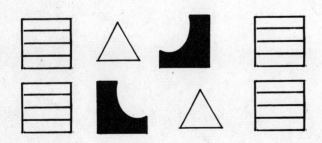

SHAPE SUBTRACTION

Cosmos and Suji are playing a shape game. Cosmos draws a picture. Then Suji erases part of the picture. What is left after Suji is done? Draw your answer. The first one is done for you.

Cosmos drew:	Suji erased:	What is left?
		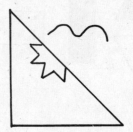

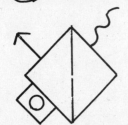	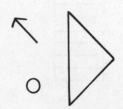	

SHAPE ADDITION

Jed and Hugh are playing a different shape game. Jed draws a picture. Then Hugh adds something to the picture. What did Hugh add to each one? Draw your answer in the middle column. The first one is done for you.

Jed drew: Hugh added: The new picture:

VERONICA'S STACK PUZZLE

Veronica has a puzzle for you. She has stacked different shapes on top of each other. Can you figure out which shape is on the bottom, in the middle, or on top of each stack? The first one is done for you.

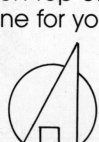
Draw the shape in the middle.

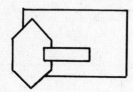
Draw the shape on top.

Draw the shape on the bottom.

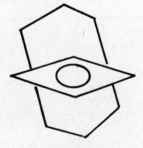
Draw the shape in the middle.

Draw the shape on the bottom.

PICTURE DETECTIVE

Milo is studying three strange drawings that he found on the sidewalk. Help Milo describe each picture. What shapes do you see? How many of each shape are there? Write a description of each drawing on the lines.

_____

_____

_____

_____

_____

_____

_____

_____

_____

MONSTER MINI-PUTT

The monsters are playing mini-putt. Each time they hit the ball, it counts as one **stroke,** or point. Use the chart below to record how many strokes each monster got on each hole.

- Veronica hit the ball twice on hole number 1, once on hole number 2, and three times on hole number 3.
- Hugh hit the ball three times on hole number 1, twice on hole number 2, and four times on hole number 3.
- Babs hit the ball once on hole number 1, twice on hole number 2, and twice on hole number 3.

Player	Hole 1	Hole 2	Hole 3	Total
Veronica				
Hugh				
Babs				

The winner is the monster with the **lowest** total score. Who won? _____

BUTTON SALE

Mrs. Trogman sells buttons. Today, she has a sale on packages that contain an even number of buttons. But some packages that contain an odd number of buttons have been put out by mistake. Circle the packages that contain an even number of buttons. Put an **X** on the packages that contain an odd number of buttons.

How many packages are actually on sale?

_____

Hint: An **even** number can be broken into two equal parts. An **odd** number cannot be broken into two equal parts.

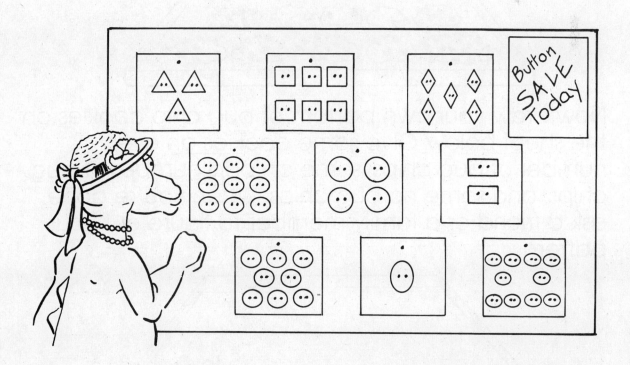

COOKIE PATTERN

Ursula baked some bug chip cookies. Then she arranged them on a cookie sheet to make a pattern. What is the pattern? To find out:

- Color cookies with an even number of bug chips red.
- Color cookies with an odd number of bug chips blue.
- Color cookies with no bug chips yellow.

Now draw your own pattern of bug chip cookies on the sheet below. Give some cookies an even number of bug chips, some an odd number of bug chips, and some no bug chips. When you're done, ask a friend or a family member to figure out your pattern.

THE SECRET PLACE

Jag wrote a secret message to Rodney. To figure out the message, first answer the questions below.

What number is in the tens' place in 568? _____

What number is in the ones' place in 174? _____

What number is in the hundreds' place in 329? _____

What number is in the tens' place in 993? _____

Use the code below to match each answer to a letter. Then unscramble the letters and write them on the lines below to finish the message.

8 = O	6 = R	1 = E
9 = K	2 = C	3 = P
5 = U	4 = A	7 = N

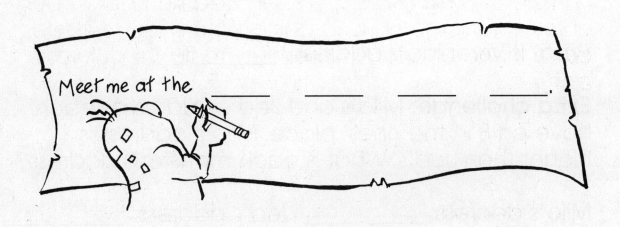

Meet me at the ____ ____ ____ ____.

VERONICA'S HOUSE

Where does Veronica live? Use the clues to find the address of her house. Color her house orange.

- Veronica's address is below 500.
- Veronica's address has a 4 in the hundreds' place.
- Veronica's address is an even number.
- The sum of the numbers in Veronica's address is less than 10.

What is Veronica's address? _____

Extra challenge: Milo's and Jed's addresses each have an 8 in the ones' place. Milo's address is higher than Jed's. What is each monster's address?

Milo's address: _____ Jed's address: _____

RIMSLEY'S RACE NUMBER

Rimsley must paint three numbers on his go-cart so he can enter a race. He likes the numbers 5, 7, and 2. Can you make six different three-digit numbers using 5, 7, and 2? Write them on the lines. The first one is done for you.

572 _____ _____

_____ _____ _____

Extra challenge: Rimsley decided that he likes the number that has 2 hundreds and 5 ones the best. Write that number on his go-cart.

MONSTER COUNT

The monsters counted bugs for a school project. They wrote the amount for each kind of bug they counted, but the digits in the numbers got all mixed up. The order of the digits in the numbers below should make the **largest** possible number. Reorder the digits and write the correct totals in the blank spaces.

BUG CHART		
	328	
	7910	
	564	
	28076	
	752136	

The monsters also counted birds. But the digits in these numbers got all mixed up, too. The order of the digits in the numbers below should make the **smallest** possible number. Reorder the digits and write the correct totals in the blank spaces.

BIRD CHART		
	81	
	912	
	3276	
	41853	
	356124	

PIGGY BANK

Maggie has the following kinds of coins in her piggy bank:

 nickel = 5¢

 dime = 10¢

 quarter = 25¢

Help Maggie find out how much money she has by skip-counting each group of coins. This is how you skip-count nickels:

5　　　10　　　15

Now you try. Skip-count Maggie's nickels to find out how much money she has in nickels. Write the amount below each coin as you count.

___　　___　　___　　___　　___

Next, skip-count Maggie's dimes. How much money does she have in dimes? Write the amount below each coin as you count.

___ ___ ___ ___ ___ ___ ___ ___ ___

Now skip-count Maggie's quarters. Remember to write the amount below each coin as you count.

___ ___ ___

How much money does Maggie have all together? Add the amounts of all the nickels, dimes, and quarters.

nickels _____

dimes _____

quarters _____

TOTAL _____

MONSTER BUILDING

Milo's aunt lives in a big building. There are 50 apartments in the building. Each apartment has a number on the door, going from numbers 1 to 50.

How many apartments have a 0 in the number on their door?
Hint: Skip-count by tens up to 50 and write the numbers as you count.

_____

_____

Answer: _____

How many apartments have a 5 on their door as the second digit of a two-digit number?
Hint: Skip-count by fives up to 50 and write the numbers as you count.

_____

_____

Answer: _____

MONSTER CLEANUP

Hugh is walking from school to the recycling depot. He stops at every fourth stone along the path to pick up trash. Put an **X** on each object that Hugh picks up.

How many objects did Hugh pick up all together?

_____

MONSTER TRICKS

Jag made some drawings for Babs. Then Babs made a comment about each drawing. Write **true** if what Babs said is correct or **false** if what she said is wrong.

Hint: If you need help, use a ruler.

Jag's drawings:	Babs says:	True or false:

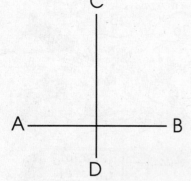

Line AB is as long as line CD. _____

Line AB is shorter than line CD. _____

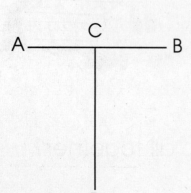

Line AB is longer than line CD. _____

24

It's Babs's turn to make drawings and Jag's turn to say something about them. Write true or false for each of Jag's comments.

Babs's drawings:	Jag says:	True or false:
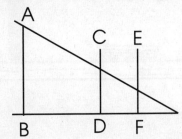	Line EF is longer than line CD.	_____
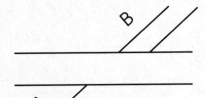	If you continued line A, it would meet line B.	_____
	The two circles are not the same size.	_____

MONSTER NUMBERS

Samantha loves big numbers. On the blackboard, she wrote the number 437. Then she broke down the number into hundreds, tens, and ones.

Help Samantha break down these numbers.

261 = _____ + _____ + _____

908 = _____ + _____ + _____

534 = _____ + _____ + _____

755 = _____ + _____ + _____

616 = _____ + _____ + _____

SUJI'S DOLLS

Suji collects stacking dolls. A stacking doll is a doll that has smaller dolls inside it. Suji has four stacking dolls. Inside two of them, there are three smaller dolls. Inside the third, there are four smaller dolls. Inside the last one, there are five smaller dolls. How many dolls does Suji have all together?

Hint: Draw the dolls that are inside each stacking doll. The first one is done for you.

Answer: Suji has _____ dolls all together.

MONSTER PRIZES

The monsters are at a game booth. They can win prizes by throwing a ball at the numbers along the wall. Which numbers did the monsters hit to win their prizes?

Ursula won a stuffed frog. She hit the number whose digits add up to 20. She hit number _____.

Rimsley won a beach ball. The number he hit is double, or two times, 22. He hit number _____.

Rodney won a baseball cap. If you subtract 15 from the number he hit, you get 72. He hit number _____.

Suji wants to win a kite. She must hit the number that can be divided into two sets of 25. She must hit number _____.

PYRAMID PUZZLES

Jag needs your help to solve the pyramid puzzles below. The two numbers on the bottom of each pyramid must add up to the number on the top. Write the missing number in each pyramid. Jag has done the first one.

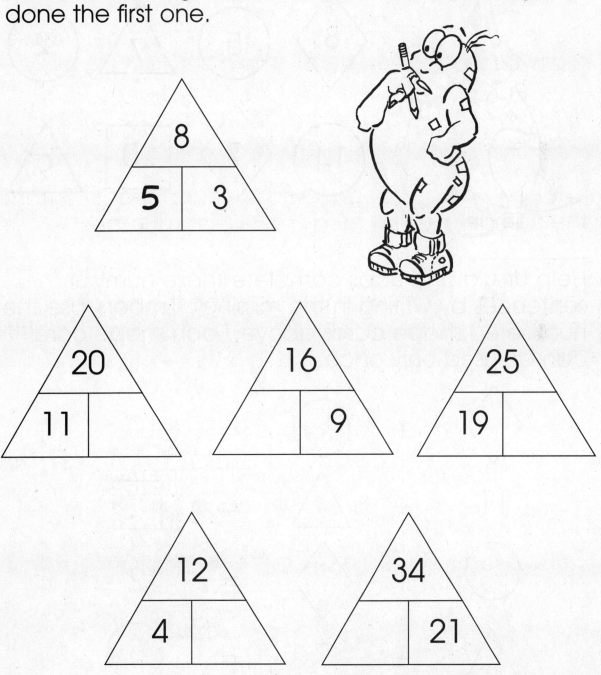

NUMBER SHAPES

Ursula and Babs are playing a number game using these numbered shape cards.

Help Ursula and Babs complete these number sentences by writing in the missing numbers. Use the numbered shape cards above. Each shape card can be used only once.

$$\diamond + \bigcirc = 10$$

$$11 + \triangle = \square$$

$$\bigcirc + \diamond = 12$$

$$\triangle + 7 = \bigcirc$$

Can you help Ursula and Babs with these subtraction problems, too? Write the missing numbers on the cards. Use the numbered shape cards below. Remember, you can use each shape card only once.

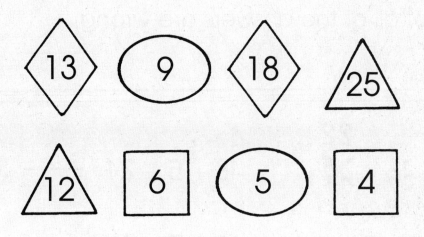

16 - □ = △

◇ - 9 = ○

△ - ○ = 20

◇ - □ = 7

MONSTER MISTAKES

The monsters tried to solve the math problems on the blackboard. But some of their answers are wrong. Mrs. Murky has already corrected one mistake. Find the other mistakes and correct them.

Hint: Not all of the answers are wrong.

10 + 12 = ~~20~~ 22   18 + 5 = 24

8 − 3 = 5   15 − 7 = 9

18 − 6 = 14   4 + 15 = 17

10 + 20 = 21   28 − 8 = 18

30 − 9 = 21   50 + 50 = 100

PICTURE PROBLEMS

Make up an addition or a subtraction problem for each monster picture. The first problem is done for you.

Problem: If each monster eats three jelly beans, how many jelly beans will be left?

Answer: _____

_____

Problem: _____

_____

_____

Answer: _____

_____

Problem: _____

_____

_____

Answer: _____

_____

Extra challenge: Make up more problems to go along with each picture!

HOW MANY WAYS?

Cosmos wants to buy an ice-cream sundae. The sundae costs 52¢. He has two quarters, four dimes, three nickels, and three pennies.

This is what each coin is worth.

25¢   10¢   5¢   1¢

Find four different ways that Cosmos can combine his coins to make 52¢. Draw the coins. Write what each coin is worth below the coin. One way to make 52¢ is done for you.

25¢ + 25¢ + 1¢ + 1¢   = 52¢

                                             = 52¢

                                             = 52¢

                                             = 52¢

Miles wants to buy a hot dog. The hot dog costs 76¢. He has three quarters, four dimes, two nickels, and six pennies. Can you find four different ways that Miles can combine his coins to make 76¢? Draw the coins. Write what each coin is worth below the coin.

= 76¢

= 76¢

= 76¢

= 76¢

MORE PICTURE PROBLEMS

Make up an addition or a subtraction problem for each monster picture. The first problem is done for you.

Problem: If the chicken lays seven more eggs, how many eggs will there be in all?

Answer: _____

_____

Problem: _____

_____

_____

Answer: _____

_____

Problem: _____

_____

_____

Answer: _____

_____

Extra challenge: Make up a multiplication problem for the last picture.

HOW HEAVY?

Hugh is comparing weights of objects. Which pairs of objects below might balance a scale? Draw lines to connect pairs of objects that weigh about the same.

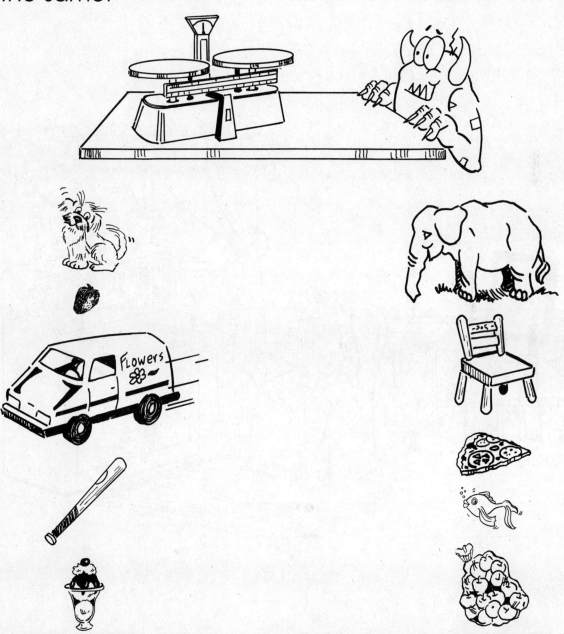

Extra challenge: Find pairs of objects in your home that weigh about the same.

MONSTER MEASURES

Some things in Veronica's room are about the same length and some things are about the same height. Draw lines to connect pairs of objects that measure about the same.

Extra challenge: Find some things in your room that are about as long as a ruler.

HOW OLD?

Minnie, Didi, Felix, and Rocky are monster pets. How old is each pet? Use the clues to find out.

- Didi's age is half of 16.
- Felix is two years older than Didi.
- Minnie is half as old as Felix.
- All together, the ages of the four pets add up to 26.

Write the age of each monster pet.

Minnie: _____

Didi: _____

Felix: _____

Rocky: _____

RODNEY'S INVENTION

Rodney invented an amazing math machine! The machine has four buttons on it. If you push the buttons, this is what the machine does:

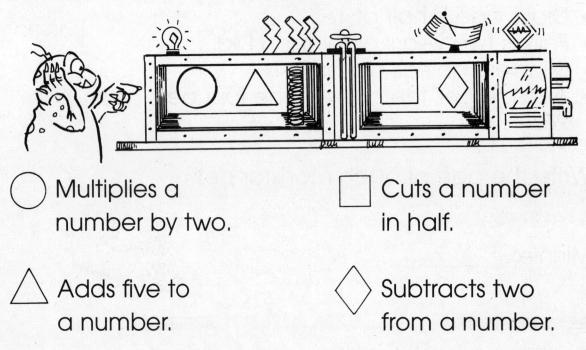

◯ Multiplies a number by two.

▢ Cuts a number in half.

△ Adds five to a number.

◇ Subtracts two from a number.

Can you figure out which button Rodney pushed to change each number in the first column below into the number in the second column? Draw the shape of the button as your answer. The first one is done for you.

Button Pushed

18	⟶	9	▢
16	⟶	14	
6	⟶	12	
26	⟶	31	

You can push as many buttons as you want on the math machine. Which buttons did Rodney push to change the numbers in each row below? Draw the shapes of the buttons in the spaces. The first one is done for you.

	Button		Button		Button
30 ⟶ 15	▢ ⟶	20	△ ⟶	18	◇
50 ⟶ 100	⟶	50	⟶	55	
24 ⟶ 22	⟶	44	⟶	49	
61 ⟶ 66	⟶	33	⟶	31	
18 ⟶ 36	⟶	34	⟶	17	
7 ⟶ 14	⟶	19	⟶	24	

MIXED-UP TIME

Mr. Tick sells clocks in his shop. Look at each clock carefully. There are two mistakes on each one. Use a pencil to correct each mistake.

Extra challenge: Look at the time on the digital clock. Draw hands on the round clock to show the same time.

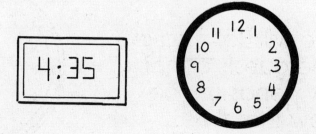

PARTY TIME!

Babs is calling her friends to invite them to a party. She wants to know what time each of them can arrive. She has found out that:

- Ursula can come at half past six.
- Rodney can arrive one and a half hours after Ursula.
- Jed can be there a half hour before Rodney.
- Suji can come two hours before Rodney.

Write the time when each monster can be at the party.

Suji: _____   Ursula: _____

Jed: _____   Rodney: _____

At what time will Babs have at least three guests at her party? Draw hands on the clock to show that time.

NUMBER CROSSWORD

Jag needs your help with this crossword puzzle. Read the clues below. Then write each answer in the squares.

Across
2. Half of a dozen.
3. It has 24 hours.
6. The highest number on a clock.

Down
1. The number of seconds in one minute.
3. Paper money that equals 100 pennies.
4. A pair.
5. It has 12 months.

A BUSY WEEK

Rimsley has lots of activities planned for this week. Help him organize his schedule. Write each activity beside the correct day in his weekly calendar.

- He has a monster scout meeting at the end of the week.
- He is going to the library in the middle of the week.
- He is playing baseball the day after Sunday.
- He is visiting his grandfather the day before Saturday.
- He has a guitar lesson the day after the baseball game.
- He is going to a movie at the beginning of the week.
- He is going to the skating rink two days after his guitar lesson.

Sunday	
Monday	
Tuesday	
Wednesday	
Thursday	
Friday	
Saturday	

CLASS PICNIC

Mrs. Murky has picked a date for her class to go on a picnic. Can you figure out what the date is? Follow the clues below. Put an **X** on each date on the calendar that you **eliminate,** or do not think is correct.

- It is not on a Friday.
- It is not on a day with an odd number.
- It is on a day with a two-digit number.
- It is on a day with a zero in the number.
- It is not on a weekend.

The picnic is on June _____.

JUNE

SUNDAY	MONDAY	TUESDAY	WEDNESDAY	THURSDAY	FRIDAY	SATURDAY
					1	2
3	4	5	6	7	8	9
10	11	12	13	14	15	16
17	18	19	20	21	22	23
24	25	26	27	28	29	30

MATH PATH

Millie needs your help to get to the Green Swamp. Use the clues below to find a path through the numbers. Color the boxes that contain the answers to the clues.

- The number in the hundreds' place in 842.

- The number of the hour that is midnight.

- The answer to 28 – 11.

- The number of nickels in a quarter.

- The total of two dozen eggs.

- The number that is half of 30.

- The number that is the double of nine.

- The last page number in this book.

17	18	27	6
4	24	39	20
2	12	15	64
19	3	60	8
62	25	10	5

OPPOSITES

The monsters are learning about **opposite images.** Opposite images are pairs of pictures that have their light and dark areas reversed, or in the opposite place.

Help the monsters choose the opposite image of each picture in column 1 from the pictures in columns 2, 3, and 4. Draw a circle around your choice. The first one is done for you.

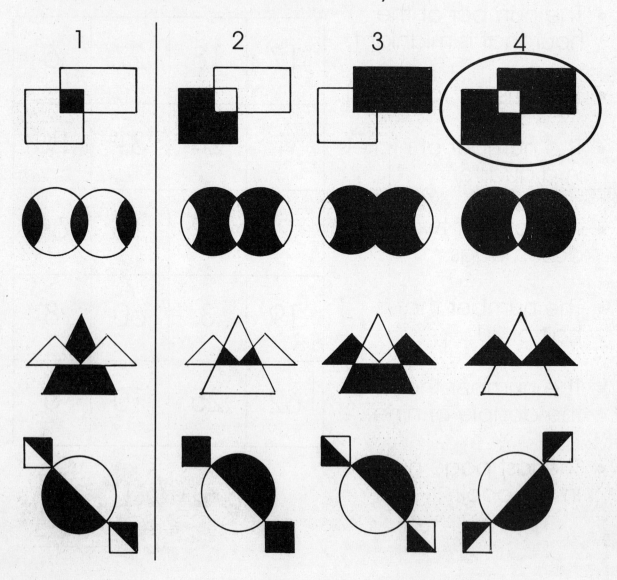

ANALOGY PUZZLES

Some puzzles are called **analogies**. An analogy compares pairs of objects to show how they are similar. Here is an example:

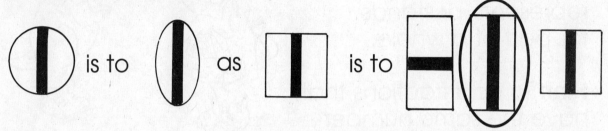

Help the monsters figure out the analogies below. Draw a circle around the figure that best completes each analogy.

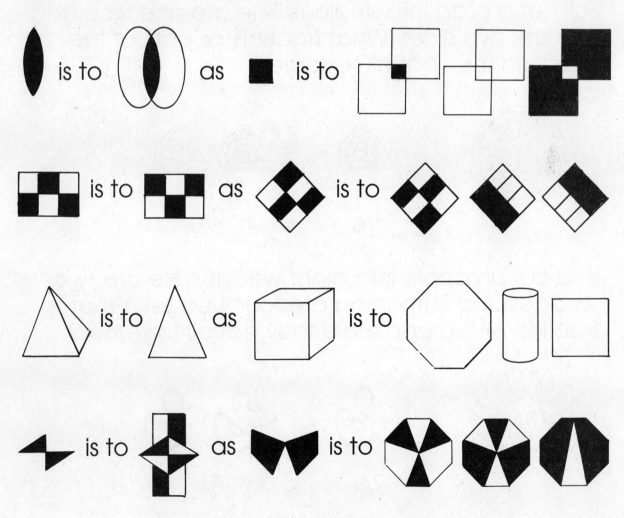

FRACTION ACTION

Help the monsters solve the **fraction** problems below. A fraction represents, or stands for, part of a whole.

Hint: To add fractions that have the same number on the bottom, add only the numbers on the top.

Suji cut a pizza into six slices. She ate one slice and Jag ate two slices. What fraction, or part, of the pizza did they eat all together?

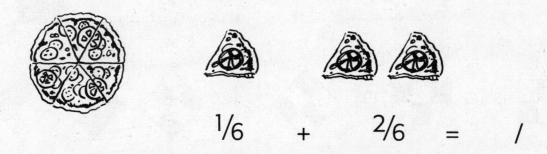

1/6   +   2/6   =   /

Jed cut an apple into eight wedges. He ate two wedges and Samantha ate four wedges. What fraction of the apple did they eat all together?

2/8   +   4/8   =   /

MORE FRACTIONS

Veronica is taking things off the table. Look at the fractions around the table. They tell you how many things she took from each group of objects. Put an **X** on all the things she took.

Hint: The total for each group of objects is the same as the number that appears on the bottom of the fraction.

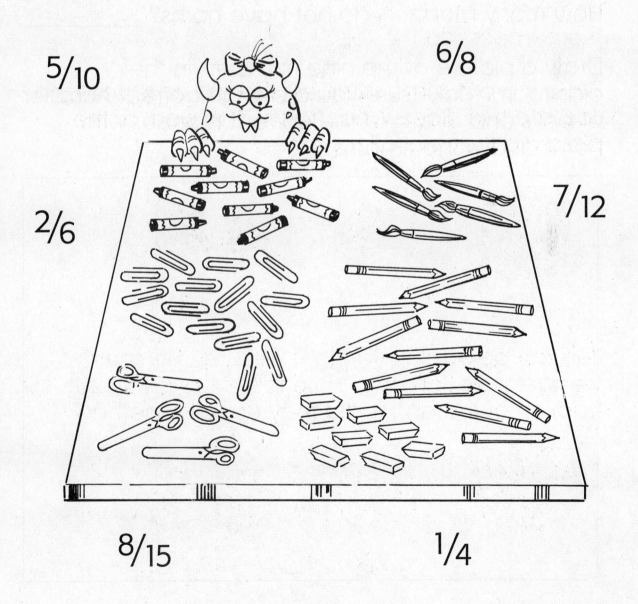

5/10

6/8

2/6

7/12

8/15

1/4

HOW MANY?

Nine monsters are in their classroom at school.

There are twice as many boys as there are girls.
How many boys are there? _____
How many girls are there? _____

Two of the girls and half of the boys have horns.
How many monsters have horns? _____
How many monsters do not have horns? _____

Draw a picture of the nine monsters in their classroom. Make sure you draw the correct number of boys and girls, and the correct number with horns and without horns.

COSMOS'S HOUSE

Cosmos drew the shapes of the rooms in his house on the grid below. Which two rooms are the same size?

_____

_____

Hint: Count the squares in each room. Two half-squares equal one whole square. Write the number of squares inside the room.

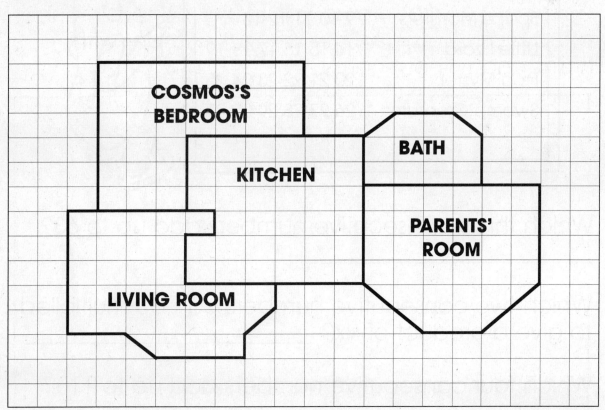

Extra challenge: If one square equals one square foot, what is the **area,** or size, of the whole house? _____ square feet

MATH WIZ

Hugh loves to make up puzzles about numbers. He is looking at a movie schedule, and he thinks he has some number puzzles for you using the dates.

Hint: Consecutive numbers are numbers that follow each other in order, such as 14, 15, and 16.

Movie	January Schedule
Bug Invasion	1 2 3 4 5 6 7 8
Space Monsters	9 10 11 12 13
Little Lizard	14 15 16 17 18 19
Frog Mystery	20 21 22 23 24 25
Swamp Creature	26 27 28 29 30 31

Which three consecutive numbers add up to 63?

_____

Which two consecutive numbers can be multiplied to give a product of six? _____

Which four consecutive numbers add up to 118?

_____

Which two consecutive numbers can be multiplied to give a product of 90? _____

54

SWEET STRAWBERRIES

Jag picked 15 strawberries from the strawberry patch. On the way home, he stopped three times to sit and rest. Each time he stopped, he ate three strawberries. How many strawberries did he have when he got home?

Jag had _____ strawberries.

Extra challenge: Write a multiplication number sentence describing how many strawberries Jag ate.

_____

MONSTER BOOK DRIVE

Babs, Rimsley, and Ursula collected books for the library. Each monster went to houses in different neighborhoods to ask for used books.

Color the map on the next page to show each monster's neighborhood for the book drive. Color only the sections that have houses. Use the information below.

- Babs went to the houses along Swamp Avenue and Oak Circle. Color her area of the map green.

- Rimsley went to the houses along Lizard Street and Gator Road. Color his area of the map red.

- Ursula went to the houses along Bug Drive, Frog Street, and Toad Road. Color her area of the map yellow.

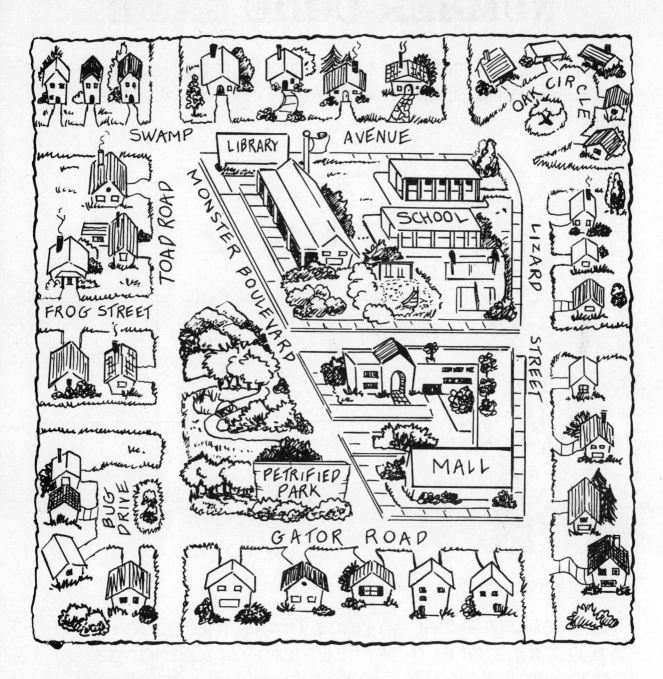

If each house donated two books to the library, how many books did each monster collect?

Babs: _____   Rimsley: _____   Ursula: _____

How many books did the monsters collect all together? _____

NUMBER-CODE GAME

Millie and Rodney are playing a number-code game. The numbers are placed in a tic-tac-toe grid like this:

1	2	3
4	5	6
7	8	9

The lines around each number are the code symbol for that number. The game is to change code symbols back into numbers. For example:

is ___95___

Help Millie and Rodney change the code symbols below into numbers. Use the tic-tac-toe grid on page 58 as a guide.

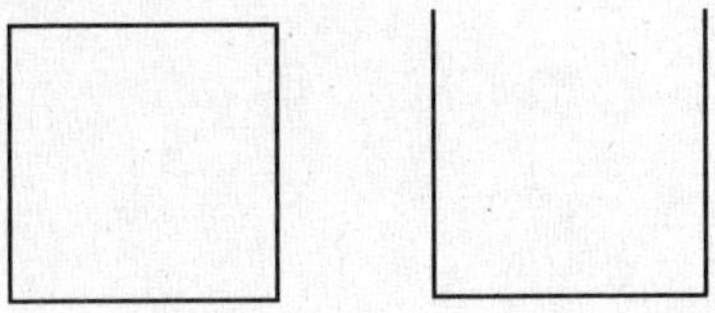

is _____

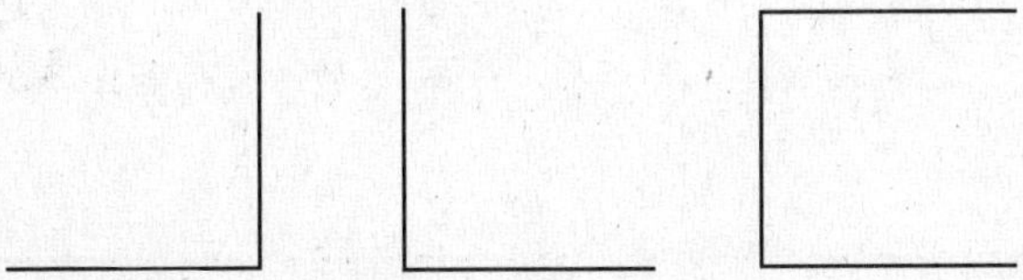

is _____

is _____

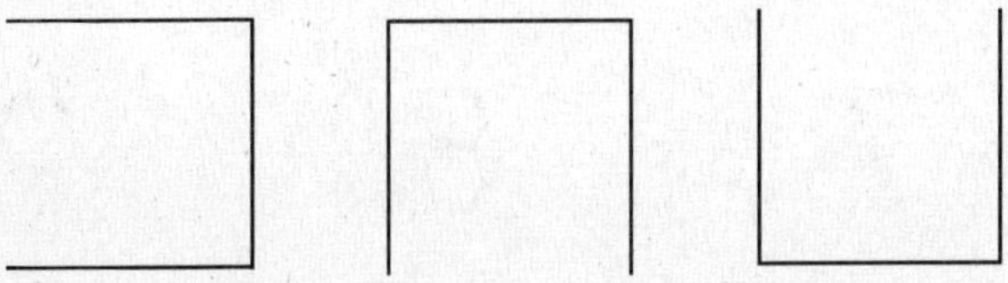

is _____

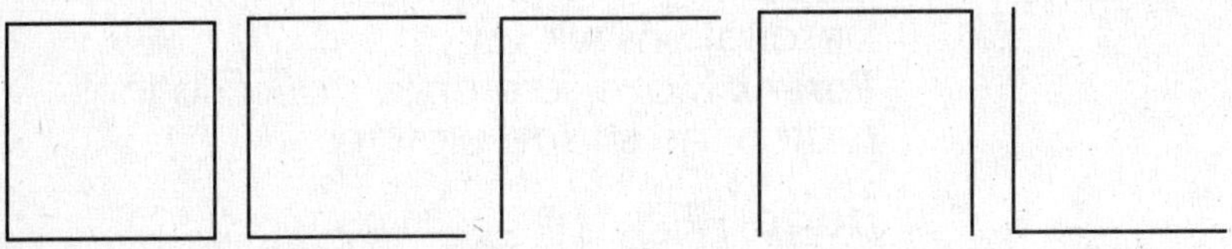

is _____

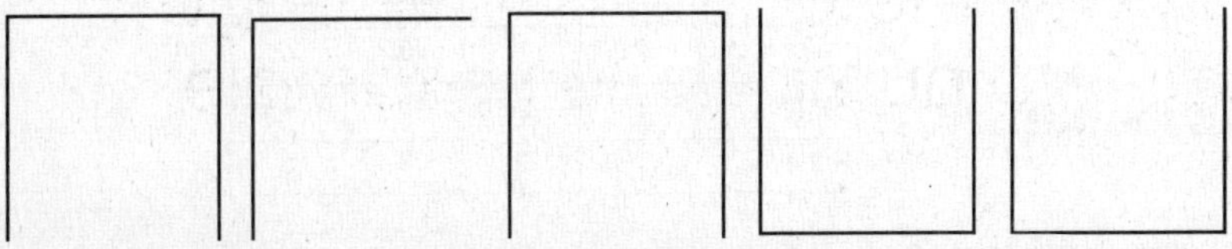

is _____

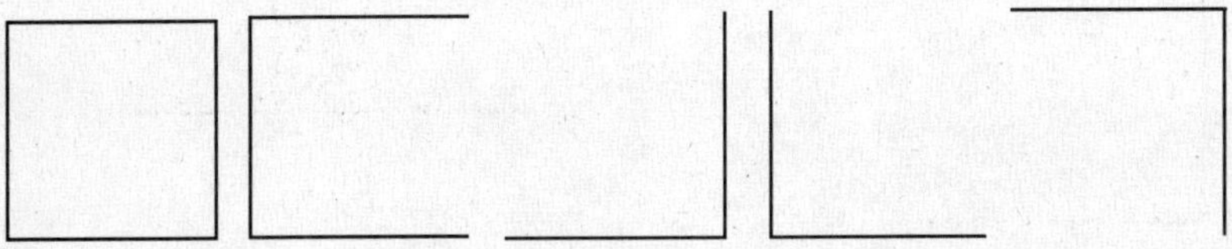

is _____

ANSWERS

page 4

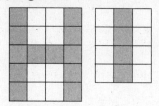

page 5

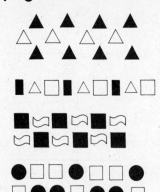

pages 6–7

Parent: Make sure child draws shapes that continue the patterns.

page 8

page 9

page 10

page 11

Descriptions will vary.
Parent: Make sure child's descriptions match the shape pictures.

page 12

Player	Hole 1	Hole 2	Hole 3	Total
Veronica	2	1	3	6
Hugh	3	2	4	9
Babs	1	2	2	5

Babs won.

page 13

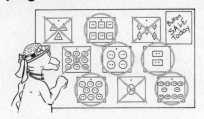

5 packages are on sale.

page 14

red – R   blue – B   yellow – Y

B R B R B
B Y B Y B
B R B R B

Child's pattern of cookies will vary.

page 15

6 in the tens' place
4 in the ones' place
3 in the hundreds' place
9 in the tens' place
6 = R   3 = P
4 = A   9 = K
Meet me at the PARK.

page 16

Veronica's address is 402.
Extra challenge: Milo's address is 498.
Jed's address is 118.

page 17

572, 527, 752, 725, 257, 275
Extra challenge: *Parent:* Child should write 275 on the go-cart.

pages 18–19

Bug Chart: 832, 9710, 654, 87620, 765321
Bird Chart: 18, 129, 2367, 13458, 123456

pages 20–21

nickels: 5, 10, 15, 20, 25
dimes: 10, 20, 30, 40, 50, 60, 70, 80, 90
quarters: 25, 50, 75
25¢ + 90¢ + 75¢ = 190¢ or $1.90

page 22

10, 20, 30, 40, 50
5 apartments have a 0 in their number.

5, 10, 15, 20, 25, 30, 35, 40, 45, 50
4 apartments have a 5 as the second digit of a 2-digit number (15, 25, 35, and 45).

page 23

Hugh picked up objects at stones number 4, 8, 12, 16, 20, 24, 28, 32, 36, and 40.
He picked up 10 objects all together.

pages 24–25

True.
False. Line AB and line CD are the same length.
False. Line AB and line CD are the same length.

False. Line CD and line EF are the same length.
True.
False. The circles are the same size.

page 26

261 = 200 + 60 + 1
908 = 900 + 0 + 8
534 = 500 + 30 + 4
755 = 700 + 50 + 5
616 = 600 + 10 + 6

page 27

Suji has 19 dolls all together.

page 28

Ursula hit number 6842.
Rimsley hit number 44.
Rodney hit number 87.
Suji must hit number 50.

page 29

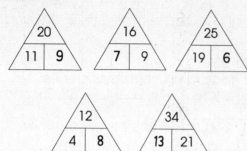

pages 30–31

$8 + 2 = 10$

$11 + 9 = 20$

$5 + 7 = 12$

$7 + 7 = 14$

$16 - 4 = 12$

$18 - 9 = 9$

$25 - 5 = 20$

$13 - 6 = 7$

page 32

$18 + 5 = 23$ (not 24)
$15 - 7 = 8$ (not 9)
$18 - 6 = 12$ (not 14)
$4 + 15 = 19$ (not 17)
$10 + 20 = 30$ (not 21)
$28 - 8 = 20$ (not 18)

$8 - 3 = 5$, $30 - 9 = 21$, and $50 + 50 = 100$ are correct.

page 33

Answer: 10 jelly beans
Problems will vary. Sample problems:
If each monster eats 3 cookies, how many will be left? Answer: 3.
If Millie catches three more butterflies than Cosmos caught, how many butterflies will she have?
Answer: 6.
Extra challenge: Problems will vary.

pages 34–35

Combinations that add up to 52¢ include:
– 1 quarter, 2 dimes, 1 nickel, 2 pennies
– 4 dimes, 2 nickels, 2 pennies
– 1 quarter, 1 dime, 3 nickels, 2 pennies

Combinations that add up to 76¢ include:
– 3 quarters, 1 penny
– 2 quarters, 2 dimes, 1 nickel, 1 penny
– 1 quarter, 4 dimes, 2 nickels, 1 penny
– 1 quarter, 4 dimes, 1 nickel, 6 pennies
Parent: Make sure child draws the correct number of each coin and writes each coin's correct value below it.

page 36

Answer: 11 eggs
Problems will vary. Sample problems:
It the monsters find 8 more shells in the sand, how many shells will there be in all? Answer: 13.
If each monster picks 2 more flowers, how many flowers will be left? Answer: 2.
Extra challenge: Sample multiplication problem: $2 \times 2 = 4$ (then, $6 - 4 = 2$).

page 37

Lines should be drawn to connect the following pairs of objects:
– the dog and the chair
– the strawberry and the goldfish
– the van and the elephant
– the baseball bat and the bag of apples
– the ice-cream sundae and the slice of pizza
Extra challenge: Results will vary.

page 38

Lines should be drawn to connect the following pairs of objects:
– the photo in the frame and the mirror (similar height)
– the lamp and the vase (similar height)
– the pencil and the scissors (similar length)
– the paper clip and the eraser (similar length)
Extra challenge: Results will vary.

page 39

Minnie: 5 years old
Didi: 8 years old
Felix: 10 years old
Rocky: 3 years old

pages 40–41

page 42

The following mistakes should be corrected:
grandfather clock: the 6 is backward; there is a 0 where the 12 should be
large clock: the minute hand is missing; there is a 6 where the 9 should be
cuckoo clock: there is an 11 where the 1 should be; there is a 0 where the 10 should be
alarm clock: there is a 13 where the 1 should be; the 3 is backward
Parent: Make sure child properly corrects each mistake.
Extra challenge:

page 43

Suji: 6:00   Ursula: 6:30
Jed: 7:30   Rodney: 8:00
Babs will have at least 3 guests at 7:30.

page 44

page 45

Sunday – movie
Monday – baseball
Tuesday – guitar lesson
Wednesday – library
Thursday – skating
Friday – visit grandfather
Saturday – monster scout meeting

page 46

The picnic is on June 20.

page 47

hundreds' place in 842 is **8**
midnight is **12**
28 – 11 is **17**
nickels in a quarter is **5**
two dozen is **24**
half of 30 is **15**
double of nine is **18**
last page number is **64**

17	18	27	6
4	24	39	20
2	12	15	64
19	3	60	8
62	25	10	5

page 48

page 49

page 50

3/6 of the pizza

6/8 of the apple

page 51

10 crayons: cross out 5 (5/10)
6 paintbrushes: cross out 2 (2/6)
15 paper clips: cross out 8 (8/15)
12 pencils: cross out 7 (7/12)
4 pairs of scissors: cross out 1 pair (1/4)
8 erasers: cross out 6 (6/8)

page 52

There are 6 boys.
There are 3 girls.
5 monsters have horns.
4 monsters do not have horns.
Parent: Make sure child's drawing matches the information above.

page 53

Cosmos's bedroom is 30 squares.
The living room is 30 squares.
The kitchen is 35 squares.
The bath is 11 squares.
The parents' bedroom is 32 squares.
Cosmos's bedroom and the living room are the same size.
Extra challenge: 138 square feet

page 54

20, 21, 22
2, 3
28, 29, 30, 31
9, 10

page 55

Jag had 6 strawberries.
Extra challenge: 3 x 3 = 9

pages 56–57

Parent: Make sure child colors the map according to the information.

Babs: 24 books
Rimsley: 24 books
Ursula: 18 books
The monsters collected 66 books all together.

pages 58–59

52
136
757
482
56983
89822
56137

the end